MW00903643

21
55

Raptors
44

Toronto Raptors

Michael E. Goodman

CREATIVE EDUCATION

Published by Creative Education
123 South Broad Street, Mankato, Minnesota 56001
Creative Education is an imprint of The Creative Company

Designed by Rita Marshall

Photos by: Allsport Photography, Associated Press/Wide World Photos, Focus on Sports, NBA Photos, UPI/Corbis-Bettmann, and SportsChrome.

Photo page 1: Marcus Camby
Photo title page: Hubert Davis

Printed in the United States of America.

Library of Congress Cataloging-in-Publication Data

Goodman, Michael E.
Toronto Raptors / Michael E. Goodman.
p. cm. — (NBA today)
Summary: Highlights the history, key players, and coaches of this NBA expansion team.
ISBN 0-88682-894-5

1. Toronto Raptors (Basketball team)—History—Juvenile literature.
[1. Toronto Raptors (Basketball team)—History. 2. Basketball—History.]
I. Title. II. Series: NBA today (Mankato, Minn.)

GV885.52.T67G66 1997 97-6651
796.323'64'09713541—dc21

First edition

5 4 3 2 1

The city of Toronto began as a small fort established by the British on the shore of Lake Ontario in 1793. It was built to protect against a possible invasion of Canada by forces of the newly independent United States of America. The invasion never occurred, but its threat led the governor of the province of Upper Canada (now known as Ontario) to move the provincial capital from Niagara, which was right on the border between Canada and the U.S., to Toronto. The tiny fortress quickly grew into a small city and eventually into one of North America's major financial, commercial,

Veteran center John Salley.

and manufacturing hubs with a population of nearly four million people.

B. J. Armstrong, the Raptors' first player, was traded before playing a game in a Toronto uniform.

Today, Toronto is also an important cultural and athletic center. It is home to Canada's best known symphony orchestra, opera company, and ballet troupe; several outstanding colleges and universities; the two-time major league baseball champion Toronto Blue Jays; and two of the most famous architectural structures in North America—the CN Tower, the world's tallest self-supporting building (at 1,815 feet high), and SkyDome, a remarkable athletic stadium. A third exciting new structure is the Air Canada Centre, designed as the home for the Toronto Raptors basketball team, one of the National Basketball Association's (NBA) newest franchises.

The Raptors made their own "invasion" of Canada at the beginning of the 1995–96 season and took the country by storm. Crowds poured into SkyDome to see the club's home games and to cheer for Toronto's newest hero, Damon Stoudamire, the NBA's top rookie in 1995–96. Stoudamire and his teammates didn't win a lot of games in their first year in the league, but they did win over a lot of Canada's die-hard hockey fans, turning them on to basketball as well. Those fans have become more sophisticated about the sport since that first season and are waiting impatiently for the chance to cheer an NBA contender in the near future.

Reviving Basketball's Canadian Roots

While hockey is Canada's national sport, basketball also has important roots north of the United States, and particularly in Ontario. Dr. James Naismith, who invented

Top gun guard/forward Doug Christie.

Raptors

the game in Springfield, Massachusetts, in 1891, was born in Almonte, Ontario. (To honor him, the Raptors play Canada's other NBA club, the Vancouver Grizzlies, every year during the preseason to see which team will win the Naismith Cup.) Even the organization of the NBA can be traced to Toronto. On November 1, 1946, the Toronto Huskies and New York Knickerbockers of the new Basketball Association of America (BAA)—which later became the NBA—competed in the league's first game in Maple Leaf Gardens in Toronto. The Knicks won that contest in a thriller, 68–66. The Huskies completed their inaugural season with a 22–38 record, and even went 15–15 at home, but not enough fans came out to support the club—it went out of business after only one year. It would take 48 years before another Toronto NBA team took to the hardwood.

1 9 9 5

In a game against Seattle, Tracy Murray scored 16 points in just one quarter of play.

The driving force behind the effort to win a new NBA franchise for the city of Toronto was local businessman John Bitove Jr. Bitove had been an excellent basketball player in high school and captained his college team to a Canadian regional championship. After that, he headed to graduate school at Indiana University. Bitove not only earned a business degree at Indiana, but also saw the Hoosiers basketball team, led by All-American guard Isiah Thomas, capture the 1981 NCAA national championship. Thomas left Indiana for the NBA following that championship season, and Bitove soon returned to Toronto to open a highly successful investing firm. During the next dozen years, Bitove watched Thomas become an NBA star, leading the Detroit Pistons to two league titles, and he became more determined than ever to find a way to bring an NBA team to his city.

Bitove told friends that he had three goals connected with bringing an NBA franchise to Toronto. "Seeing kids play the greatest sport ever invented, making the community a better place to live, and winning an NBA championship is what it's all about," he said.

The biggest hurdle Bitove faced was convincing league officials that a city outside of the United States—even one as big as Toronto—could support an NBA club. The league agreed to hold exhibition games in SkyDome in 1989 and 1992. Each attracted more than 25,000 fans—proof that Canadian sports fans were eager for NBA basketball to be revived in their country.

Oliver Miller set a Raptors record with 17 rebounds in a game against Washington.

In July 1993, an NBA expansion committee came to Toronto to meet with Bitove and his partners as well as several other groups of business people interested in bidding for a new franchise. Bitove's group had some interesting ideas, including building a new arena in downtown Toronto. The proposed building site was close to major businesses, whose help would be needed to support the team financially, and near a subway line that would provide easy access for fans, even in the winter. The NBA Board of Governors liked Bitove's ideas. In November 1993 his group was awarded the right to establish the league's 28th club starting in the 1995–96 season.

The first step had been taken, but there was still much to be done before a Toronto team could take the court for its first NBA game.

For one thing, the team needed an attractive name and symbol to encourage fans to support the new franchise. The club's management announced a nationwide "Name Game,"

Damon Stoudamire, one of the NBA's best young point guards.

Ed Pinckney, contributing off the bench.

and more than 2,000 entries poured in to Bitove's offices over the next few months. The list was whittled down to several animal names such as Beavers, Bobcats, Scorpions, Raptors, and T-Rex., with Raptors winning out. A new logo was designed featuring an aggressive, sharp-toothed little dinosaur dribbling a basketball. The image caught on quickly throughout Canada and the United States. More than $20 million in Raptors clothing and sports gear was sold in just the first month it went on the market.

1 9 9 6

Acie Earl scored a career-high 40 points competing against his old team, the Celtics.

At the same time, the club began selling season tickets at SkyDome for its 41 home games during the 1995–96 season. Sales were brisk, and by the end of 1994 deposits for season's tickets were received from more than 15,000 eager Canadian basketball fans.

The incredible response from all over the country excited Bitove and convinced him that he had been right about bringing professional basketball to Canada. "It's the most rewarding feeling," commented Bitove, "watching people, many of whom have never seen or heard a basketball game in their lives, take hold of the sport so passionately."

ISIAH COMES ON BOARD

The Raptors were already a hit off the court, but they still needed a coach and players to perform on the court. Bitove focused next on putting together the team's first roster. He knew he was going to need help with the task, and he had just the right basketball leader in mind—his former hero at Indiana University, Isiah Thomas. Thomas had recently retired after an outstanding 13-year NBA career with the Detroit Pistons, during which he earned 12 All-Star team selections, two NBA championship rings, and a berth on Dream Team II that took part in the 1994 World Basketball Championships played in Toronto. Thomas had many qualities that led Bitove to name him the club's executive vice president of basketball operations—he was a proven leader, he understood how to win in the NBA, and he had learned patience being part of a Detroit franchise that had progressed from the bottom of the league to the top during his years with the team. Thomas understood firsthand that it might take several seasons to build the Raptors into a winner, and he was willing to go through all of the growing pains the new club might face.

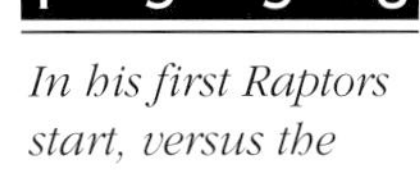

In his first Raptors start, versus the Pistons, Sharone Wright led the club with 25 points.

Thomas officially came on board in May 1994 and spent the 1994–95 season scouting the NBA, other pro leagues, and colleges for a coach and players for the new team. In May 1995, the Raptors held a free-agent camp at Seneca College near Toronto. Lots of former NBA players and minor leaguers showed up, hoping to win a berth with the expansion club. Thomas asked an old friend, Pistons assistant coach Brendan Malone, to run the camp. Thomas didn't spot any potential Raptors players during the tryouts, but he did find his new coach. He was so impressed with how well Malone organized and motivated the group of free agents that he hired him to become the Raptors' first head coach.

The Raptors still had three other ways to find players to fill their roster. First, there would be an expansion draft, with each of the league's 27 existing teams making available some of its underachieving players or aging veterans for the Raptors and Vancouver Grizzlies (the other expansion team) to choose from. Second, there would be the annual draft of college players to be held at the end of June 1995 at Sky-Dome, with Toronto and Vancouver choosing near the top in each of the two rounds. The Raptors would also be able to fill roster openings by signing other players coming out of college who were not drafted or free agents who were not under contract to other NBA clubs.

Walt "The Wizard" Williams left Miami as a free agent to join the Raptors.

Thomas and Malone put their heads together to focus on the two drafts. The two men had very different points of view about the type of players they wanted to pick. Malone was interested in NBA veterans who could help the team get off to a quick start and win as many games as possible during its first year. Thomas was more interested in acquiring talented young players who might develop into stars over a period of several seasons.

The two men reached some compromises during the expansion draft. The Raptors' first selection was veteran guard B. J. Armstrong, who had played on three championship teams with the Chicago Bulls. Among other veterans picked were center John Salley, Thomas's former teammate with the Pistons; guard Willie Anderson from the San Antonio Spurs; Jerome Kersey from the Portland Trail Blazers; and Ed Pinckney from the Milwaukee Bucks. Younger players selected included centers Zan Tabak from the Houston Rockets and Acie Earl from the Boston Celtics; center-forward Oliver Miller from the Detroit Pistons; forwards Doug Smith from the Dallas Mavericks and Dontonio Wingfield from the Seattle SuperSonics; and guard B. J. Tyler from the Philadelphia 76ers. However, not all of those players actually made the Raptors' opening-night roster. Thomas engineered a number

Veteran guard Willie Anderson.

22
Raptors
22
ORKMAN
3

Powerful veteran Acie Earl.

of trades before the season began to try to put together a more balanced and competitive club.

DRAFTING "MIGHTY MOUSE"

After the expansion draft, Thomas and Malone assessed their picks and came up with the same conclusion—what the club still needed most was a point guard to run the offense. It needed someone a little like Isiah Thomas, a good floor leader who could score when needed but who also loved to pass off to his teammates. Thomas already had a player like that in mind who would probably be available in the college draft—tiny and talented Damon Stoudamire from the University of Arizona.

1996

Vincenzo Esposito netted a career-high 18 points in a game against New York.

Thomas had been scouting Stoudamire for a while. He knew that although the young man was only 5-foot-10 and weighed just 170 pounds, he had the courage to drive inside among the big men and could pop three-point shots with deadly accuracy from the outside. Often underestimated because of his size, Stoudamire had a picture of the cartoon character Mighty Mouse tattooed on his right arm. Behind the tattoo was a message: "I may be small but I'm strong and fast, and I don't let 'bad guys' stand in my way."

"Mighty Mouse was always saving people, always coming to the rescue," Stoudamire explained. "He was the man. He could get you out of any jam. That's what I always wanted to be like. Oh, and yeah, he was small."

Stoudamire played his college ball at the University of Arizona, where he was a three-time All-Pac 10 performer. He led the Wildcats to the Final Four in his junior year and to a

Brendan Malone, the Raptors' first head coach (pages 18–19).

PEPSI
Raptors
30
WHITNE

top 20 national ranking in his senior year. Yet many basketball fans didn't know that much about him, particularly fans in Canada. When NBA Commissioner David Stern announced the Raptors' first-round choice before a large crowd gathered at SkyDome on draft day, there was loud booing from the Toronto fans.

1996

Ed Pinckney had a season-high 16 rebounds in two separate games.

But the booing didn't bother the two men. "We're new, so we can try to be more innovative, take more risks," said Thomas. "Don't let his size fool you," he said of Stoudamire. "He's very strong. He has the ability to break down

Damon Stoudamire plays like an experienced veteran.

defenses, and that's what you have to have. He's not going to be a good player . . . He's going to be a great player."

"The way I saw it, they weren't booing me, because they really didn't know who I was," Stoudamire recalled. "I knew that once they saw me play, they'd like me."

Stoudamire made it easy for the fans to like him, as a person and a player. Off the court, he donated time and money to many youth organizations in the Toronto area and was rated one of the easiest players to interview by sportswriters. On the court, he led all rookies in assists, steals, and free throw percentage, while he was second to Philadelphia's Jerry Stackhouse in scoring with a 19.0 average. His 9.3 assists per game was fifth best among all guards in the league in 1995–96. The statistic that Stoudamire was the most proud of, however, was that he led all rookies in minutes played per game, proving just how durable he was. In fact, only six players in NBA history ever averaged more minutes per game in their rookie year, and they were all big, strong guys now in the NBA Hall of Fame. Following the season, Stoudamire was a runaway winner for the NBA Rookie of the Year Award.

1 9 9 6

Alvin Robertson was among the league leaders with an average 2.16 steals per game.

"Damon's tough, he's relentless," said former teammate Alvin Robertson. "He doesn't care who you are or how big you are—he just keeps pounding at you. The basketball skills are obviously there, but what sets him apart is what's in his chest. You can't put a tape measure around his heart."

Stoudamire proved his courage under fire in a game against the Chicago Bulls on March 24, 1996. The Bulls, led by Michael Jordan and Scottie Pippen, were on a record-breaking pace, having lost only seven games all season.

Tracy Murray, a scoring threat.

They certainly didn't expect the Raptors, who were 17–49 at the time, to put up much of a fight. Enter Mighty Mouse. In front of 36,131 fans at SkyDome—the most ever to watch a basketball game in Canada—Stoudamire helped keep the contest close by dishing out numerous assists and bombing in three-point shots. (He finished the game with a season-high 30 points and six three-pointers.) Heading into the last quarter, the Bulls were up by only four points, 83–79. Then Raptors forward Tracy Murray and center Oliver Miller joined Stoudamire in the offensive attack—Toronto matched Chicago basket for basket throughout the last period. The final result was an amazing 109–108 upset victory for the Raptors. Toronto fans clapped and screamed for their new heroes. Mighty Mouse had saved the day again.

1 9 9 6

Doug Christie dished out a career-best eight assists in his first start with Toronto.

Following the game, even the Bulls' players had praise for Damon Stoudamire. "Most guys with great speed can't shoot," remarked Chicago guard Steve Kerr. "Most shooters don't have the speed. Damon's got both."

"He's a tough little player," added Jordan, who had been outplayed by Stoudamire that night.

The victory over the Bulls was only one highlight of the Raptors' first season in the NBA. Toronto also recorded wins over the Orlando Magic, the second best team in the Eastern Conference, and the Seattle SuperSonics, the top team in the Western Conference. No other club in the league beat all three of those teams in the 1995–96 season.

Toronto's final record of 21–61 may not seem impressive, but it was among the best for any expansion team in NBA history and easily outdistanced the 15–67 mark recorded by the Raptors' cross-country rival, the Vancouver Grizzlies, who joined the league the same year. Even more exciting was the fact that only two other teams in the league—the Chicago Bulls and Orlando Magic—had a higher average attendance for home games during the season, and five of the seven largest crowds of the year were at SkyDome.

1 9 9 6

In a game versus Boston, Popeye Jones recorded season highs in points (22) and rebounds (21).

POPEYE AND THE "CAMBY MAN"

Isiah Thomas was happy with the Raptors' first-year performance, but he wasn't satisfied. He knew some changes were needed to improve the club's overall performance. As a result, the Toronto team that took the court to begin the 1996–97 season was very different from the one that had brought pro basketball back to Canada the year before. The team's cornerstone, Damon Stoudamire, was still there, out to prove that he belonged among the top playmakers and scorers in the NBA. But he had a completely different supporting cast. There was even a new head coach. Thomas thought that a younger man might be better able to motivate the young players on the Raptors, so he asked 35-year-old Toronto assistant coach Darrell Walker to take over the reins from Brendan Malone. In addition, Thomas hoped that Walker, who had been a defensive standout during his NBA playing career, would help turn around the Raptors' two weakest areas—rebounding and defense.

Rebounding was also the reason that Thomas made a trade with the Dallas Mavericks to obtain Ronald "Popeye" Jones for the Raptors. Jones, who got his nickname because his older brother was watching a Popeye cartoon when his mom brought him home from the hospital, had been one of only 10 NBA players to average in double figures in both scoring and rebounding during the 1995–96 season. The 6-foot-8 leaper quickly established himself as the "king of the boards" in Toronto and immediately became a big hit with the fans, too. They appreciated his hard-working style and his upbeat personality.

"I wasn't one of those high-school players who was destined for the NBA," said Jones. "I've had to work hard." Working hard meant spending a year in Europe following college, improving his game and losing 45 pounds in order to win a spot on an NBA roster. Working hard also meant changing his game from being a leading scorer at Murray State in Tennessee to focusing primarily on rebounding and defense in the pros.

1 9 9 6

In only 17 minutes, Zan Tabak scored a season-high 16 points to help beat Milwaukee.

While Popeye had gotten only a few headlines during his college days, his new partner at forward on the Raptors, Marcus Camby, was often front page news. Camby, who led the University of Massachusetts to the Final Four in 1996, won several awards as College Player of the Year following his junior season at UMass. One of those honors, the Wooden Award, recognized both Marcus's playing ability and his hard work in the classroom, where he maintained a 3.0 average. He decided to turn pro a year early in order to test his skills in the NBA.

The Raptors had the second pick in the 1996 college draft, and Thomas set his sights on Camby. "What Marcus brings to a team is unique," Thomas noted. How unique? His former college coach John Calipari, now head coach of the New Jersey Nets, said that Camby is "a seven-footer with guard skills who blocks shots."

Marcus Camby, Toronto's young threat at forward (pages 26–27).

Thomas was also attracted to Camby because of the young man's leadership, intelligence, and determination. He grew up playing basketball in housing projects in Hartford, Connecticut. There were no baskets in the neighborhood, so kids would cut the bottoms out of milk crates and hang the crates on clothesline poles. UMass had baskets and a big arena when Marcus arrived on campus, but it also had a history of mediocre basketball teams. He helped change that reputation quickly. The Minutemen were often ranked number one in the country during Marcus's years there.

1 9 9 7

In a win over the 76ers, Carlos Rogers hit his previous season's highs in points (29) and rebounds (13).

Coach Walker was thrilled to have Camby come on board in Toronto. "This guy has a lot of skills. He can pass, and he can shoot the ball pretty well. Best of all, he can block shots. That's something this team really needs."

Camby was not the only new weapon to join the Raptors. Free agent Walt Williams, an outstanding shooter and ball handler, decided to sign with Toronto and provide veteran leadership for the team. At 6-foot-8, Williams is tall enough and strong enough to play small forward, but he's also agile enough to play in the backcourt. He quickly joined with Damon Stoudamire, slashing speedster Doug Christie, and outside-shooting threat Hubert Davis to form a solid nucleus for the Raptors' offense. Backing up Popeye Jones and Marcus Camby on the boards are Carlos Rogers and Sharone Wright, both of whom are nearly seven feet tall and should develop into solid rebounders and inside scorers.

All of the Toronto players have three things in common—they are young, they are talented, and they need experience. It may take a while for the Raptors to adjust to all of the changes they have been going through and to learn to play

First-round draft pick Marcus Camby.

The versatile Walt "The Wizard" Williams.

Hubert Davis, a top three-point shooter.

together as a cohesive unit. "We need to find our chemistry and continuity," said Coach Walker. "If this team gels the way I think it can, we'll improve our rebounding, defense, and ballhandling, and we'll win some big games. I don't feel any pressure to win 35 or 40 games a season right away. My only mandate is to make sure that our young players are developing and that we are moving in the right direction."

1 9 9 7

Head coach Darrell Walker led the Raptors to a first-ever 30-win season.

The players weren't the only ones to experience change and growth within the club. At the end of the 1996-97 season, it was announced that Isiah Thomas would become majority owner of the Raptors, a move that made Thomas the first-ever black to become an owner of a pro sports team.

The experiment that John Bitove began in Toronto is turning out to be a big success. The Raptors are breaking new ground in a country once again new to the NBA, and they are rapidly convincing hockey fans that a fast break on the boards can be just as exciting as a breakaway on the ice.